YOU KNOW YOU'RE A NEBRASKAN...

YOU KNOW YOU'RE A NEBRASKAN...

... WHEN YOU APPRECIATE GOOD GRASS.

BiG BLUESTEM, BUFFALO, PRAiRiE LOVE, GRAMA.

...WHEN YOU ENJOY DRESSING FORMAL.

A NEW SEED CAP AND CLEAN OVERALLS WITH THE SIDE BUTTONS DONE UP.

...WHEN YOU KNOW SUMMER IS 8 MONTHS LONG.

...WHEN YOU AVOID USING BIG WORDS.

...WHEN YOU KNOW RAIN COMES IN HUNDREDTHS.

...WHEN YOU HATE THE DEGENERATE EAST.

...WHEN YOU'RE NOT SURPRISED IF IT'S 100° ABOVE ZERO OR 35° BELOW.

ON THE SAME DAY.

...WHEN YOU VOTE EVERY ELECTION.

BUT NEVER VOTE FOR THE SAME PERSON
TWO ELECTIONS IN A ROW.

...WHEN YOU ENJOY GOOD LITERATURE.

LIKE THE STUFF YOU PICK UP AT THE FAIR
THAT TELLS YOU ABOUT COMBINES.

... WHEN YOU CALL YOUR BROTHER IN FLORIDA WHEN IT'S 90°
THERE AND 10° BELOW HERE.

AND YOU DON'T CARE.

...WHEN YOU ONCE MET JOHNNY CARSON.

TOLD HiM TO KEEP OFF YOUR LAWN WiTH HiS BiKE.

...WHEN YOU LOVE TO VISIT THE BIG APPLE.

NEBRASKA CITY.

...WHEN 200 FRIENDS COME TO YOUR DAUGHTER'S WEDDING.

190 OF THEM IN PICKUP TRUCKS.

... WHEN YOU PREPARE FOR A BLIZZARD.

EVERY YEAR. IN AUGUST.

...WHEN YOU THINK THE STOCK MARKET DEALS MOSTLY IN BARROWS AND GILTS.

AND YOU KNOW WHAT BARROWS AND GILTS ARE.

...WHEN YOU LISTEN TO BIG JOE'S POLKA PARTY.

AND <u>KNOW</u> THE PEOPLE HE DEDICATES NUMBERS TO.

...WHEN YOU FEEL SAFE IN NEW JERSEY.

IF YOU CAN FIND KFAB ON THE DIAL.

...WHEN YOU TOUR EUROPE, AND CALL HOME EVERY NIGHT.

TO ASK IF IT RAINED.

...WHEN YOU ALWAYS TIP 15 PER CENT IN RESTAURANTS.

OR IS IT 15 CENTS?

...WHEN YOU LOOK FORWARD TO A GOURMET MEAL.

A BIG MAC WITH MUSHROOMS.

...WHEN YOU OWN A SMALL PIECE OF LAND.

FOUR SECTIONS.

...WHEN THE ONLY TIME YOU WEAR A TIE IS TO FUNERALS.

A STRING TIE.

...WHEN YOU RESERVE THE TITLE "DOCTOR" FOR PHYSICIANS AND VETERINARIANS.

AND TRUST VETERINARIANS.

... WHEN YOU CAN SAY YOU ONCE
ACTUALLY SAW A JACKALOPE.

AND SAY IT WITH A STRAIGHT FACE.

...WHEN YOU ORDER THE <u>LARGE</u> HORS D'OEUVRES PLATE.

AND EXPECT BEER NUTS, PICKLED EGGS, AND JERKY.

... iF YOU LiKE TO SKi.

AND EVEN OWN YOUR OWN BOAT.

...iF YOUR ANCESTORS CAME HERE ON THE BURLINGTON.

NOT THE MAYFLOWER.

... WHEN YOU ARE INVITED TO A COCKTAIL PARTY AT 6.

...WHEN YOU NEVER SAW A MODiGLiANi.

BUT <u>LOVE</u> RUNZAS.

...WHEN YOU CAN SAY WITH A STRAIGHT FACE THAT BAD WEATHER BUILDS CHARACTER.

LOOK AT ALL THE CHARACTERS...!

...WHEN YOU THINK THE NORMAN CONQUEST HAD SOMETHING TO DO WITH THE 1971 HUSKER-OKLAHOMA GAME.

...WHEN YOU DRIVE WITH ONE HAND AT THE TOP OF THE STEERING WHEEL.

SO YOU CAN WAVE AT OTHER DRIVERS.

... WHEN YOU ONCE SAW AN OPERA
AND REALLY ENJOYED IT.

IN NASHVILLE.

... WHEN YOU ENJOY SEAFOOD.

ROCKY MOUNTAIN OYSTERS.

...WHEN YOU LiKE TO DRiVE iN THE FAST LANE.

45 m.p.h.

...WHEN YOU ARE PROUD NEBRASKA WAS THE HOME OF WILLIAM JENNINGS BRYAN.

... WHEN YOU GO HUNTING.

WITHOUT CHANGING YOUR SHOES.

...WHEN YOU SING "GOD BLESS AMERICA".